TENNIS

A TRUE BOOK

by
Christin Ditchfield

Children's Press®
A Division of Scholastic Inc.

New York Toronto London Auckland Sydney
Mexico City New Delhi Hong Kong
Danbury, Connecticut

A junior-level
tennis player

Reading Consultant
Nanci R. Vargus, Ed.D.
Assistant Professor
Literacy Education
University of Indianapolis
Indianapolis, IN

Library of Congress Cataloging-in-Publication Data

Ditchfield, Christin.
    Tennis / by Christin Ditchfield.
        p. cm. – (A true book)
Includes bibliographical references (p.) and index.
    ISBN 0-516-22589-8 (lib. bdg.)   0-516-26960-7 (pbk.)
1. Tennis—Juvenile literature. I. Title. II. Series.
GV996.5 .D57 2003
796.342—dc21

                                    2001008504

1 2 3 4 5 6 7 8 9 10 R 12 11 10 09 08 07 06 05 04 03

Contents

How Tennis Began   5

The Rules   12

The Equipment   22

The Skills   28

Making the Team   35

To Find Out More   44

Important Words   46

Index   47

Meet the Author   48

A young player
returning a shot

How Tennis Began

Every day, millions of people around the world play tennis. It's hard to say when this popular sport began. For hundreds of years, people have enjoyed playing games with balls and paddles. In the 1200s, French athletes played *jeu de paume*—"game of the

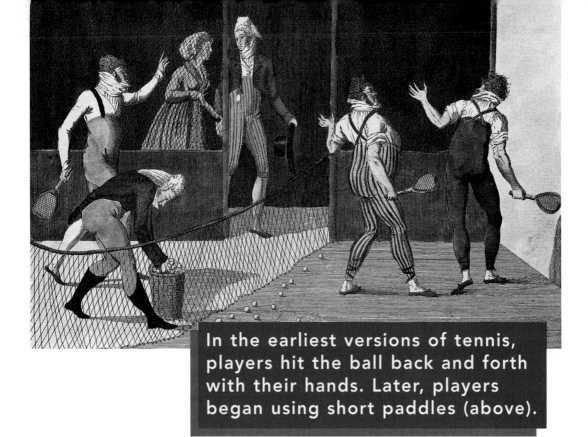

In the earliest versions of tennis, players hit the ball back and forth with their hands. Later, players began using short paddles (above).

palm." They hit a little ball back and forth with the palms of their hands. Before a player hit the ball, he called out *"Tenetz!"* or "Take heed!" It meant, "Pay attention. Play is about to begin."

This is probably where the game of "tennis" got its name.

British Army Major Walter C. Wingfield is known as the Father of Modern Tennis. In 1873, Major Wingfield decided to create a new game that men and women could enjoy together at outdoor parties. He designed special equipment and organized rules for the game he called "sphairistike." *Sphairistike* is the Greek word for "ball game." People loved Major Wingfield's game—

but they didn't like the name! Since the game was often played on grassy lawns, people began calling it "lawn tennis."

A British army officer attended one of Major Wingfield's parties. He really liked lawn tennis. When the officer moved to Bermuda, he taught the game to the people there. An American woman took a vacation in Bermuda, where she saw people playing this exciting new game. Mary Outerbridge decided to teach the game to her friends in

An illustration showing people playing lawn tennis in England in 1874

New York. Mary's family owned the Staten Island Cricket and Baseball Club. They built the first tennis courts in the United States.

Less than ten years after Major Wingfield invented lawn tennis, it had spread all over the world. By 1881, there were thirty-three tennis clubs in the United States. They joined together to form the United States Lawn Tennis Association (now the United States Tennis Association). They began organizing local, national, and even international tennis competitions.

Today, tennis isn't a party game. It's a fast-paced,

Today, people of all ages enjoy playing tennis.

competitive sport. People of all ages and abilities enjoy playing tennis. Some play for fun or exercise. Others play for the thrill of competition—the excitement that comes with winning a big match!

The Rules

Tennis players compete on a long, rectangular field called a "court." The court's surface may be hardcourt (a concrete-like surface), grass, clay, or even carpet. A tennis court measures 78 feet (24 meters) long and 36 feet (11 m) wide. Painted white lines mark the

The famous tennis courts at Wimbledon, in England, have a grass surface.

boundaries of the court. A 3.5-foot- (1-meter-) tall net divides the court in half.

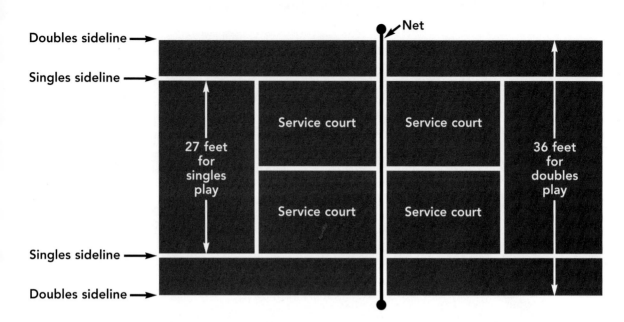

Doubles sideline →
Singles sideline →
Net
27 feet for singles play
Service court
Service court
Service court
Service court
36 feet for doubles play
Singles sideline →
Doubles sideline →

The boundaries of a tennis court are wider for doubles games than for singles games.

In a singles match, one player competes against another player. In a doubles match, a team of two players competes against another team of two players.

Tennis is scored in points, games, and sets. The first player (or team) to win four points wins a game. However, if the two sides are tied at three points each, they must keep playing until one side wins two points more than the other.

When players have won at least six games and at least two more than their **opponents**, they win a set. To win a match, players must win two out of three sets or three out of five sets.

The main goal in tennis is to hit a shot that your opponent can't return.

A player wins a point by hitting a shot that an opponent cannot return. A player's opponent wins a point when the player hits the ball into the net or outside the boundary lines on the court.

Tennis has an unusual way of keeping score. A score of zero points is called "love." The player who wins the first point has a score of "15." If each player wins a point, the score is 15-15 or "15-all." A player who has won two points has a score

A tennis scoreboard

of "30." Winning a third point gives the player a score of "40." If both players are tied at 40-40, the score is called "deuce." Since players must win each game by two points, they keep playing that game until one player has won two more points than the other player.

A tennis match begins with one player hitting or "serving" the ball across the net. The ball must land within the lines of the "service court" on the other side of the net and

A serve is always aimed for the service court across the net and diagonal from the server.

diagonal from the server. If the ball misses the service court, the shot is called a "fault." The player must serve again. If the player misses the second serve, her or she "double faults" and loses the point.

Sometimes a player's serve is so quick and powerful that the opponent can't return it. The server has hit an "ace." Usually, the opponent does get to the ball in time. The opponent must then return the shot into the server's court before the ball bounces twice on the opponent's side of the court.

The two players **rally** back and forth, using different types

Players rallying back and forth

of shots to keep the ball in play. A point ends when one of the players misses the ball or hits it out of bounds or into the net. Players take turns serving every other game.

The Equipment

A tennis player hits the ball with a specially designed racket. A tennis racket has a thin frame made of a lightweight material such as graphite, aluminum, fiberglass, or wood.

The racket has a handle that is wrapped in rubber or leather to cushion the player's grip. The

To play tennis, you need only a court, a racket (left), and tennis balls (above).

top of the racket, called the "head," is shaped like a circle or an oval. Rows of tightly woven strings run back and forth across the racket head.

The strings are attached to holes in the side of the frame. When strings wear out, they can be replaced with new ones.

A standard tennis ball weighs about 2 ounces (57 grams). It measures 8 inches (20 centimeters) around and 2 inches (5 cm) across. This hollow rubber ball is covered with felt—a soft, fuzzy type of cloth. Most tennis balls are yellow or white. The bright color makes it easy for players to see the ball.

In the early days of tennis, men and women played in fancy, white clothing.

A hundred years ago,
people played tennis in fancy,
formal clothes. Men wore long
pants and women wore ankle-
length dresses. These clothes
were always white. Today, most

Today, tennis players wear cool, comfortable, colorful clothes.

players wear loose, comfortable clothes that give them room to move freely. Players wear shorts and T-shirts or short-sleeved collared shirts, often in bright colors or patterns. Women sometimes wear short skirts or tennis dresses that are designed for athletic play.

All tennis players wear tennis shoes. These rubber-soled sports shoes cushion the feet as players run up and down the hard court surface. Thick socks absorb sweat and keep a player's feet from getting blisters.

The Skills

In tennis, a player's size is not as important as his or her speed. Players need quick **reflexes**— quick feet to get to the ball in time and quick hands to direct the racket and aim the shot. The goal is to win points by hitting unreturnable shots. This takes strategy, as well as strength and

Tennis players need quick reflexes to get to the ball in time (above). A tennis player must stay calm and focused (right).

power. Strategy means hitting the right shot at the right time in the right place. Tennis players must stay calm and **focused** in order to think clearly and play their best game.

Junior-level tennis players doing a practice drill

Serious players often work with coaches who help them develop their skills. They do special drills and exercises to increase their speed, strength, and **endurance**. They practice their shot-making skills daily.

All tennis players use several basic shots: the serve, the "groundstroke," the "volley," the "drop shot," the "lob," and the "smash." A powerful serve gets things started and puts the ball into play. When the

Each game starts with a serve.

A boy hitting a groundstroke (left) and a player reaching for a volley (below)

ball has bounced once, the returner hits a groundstroke to send it back over the net. If the server is close to the net, he or she may be able to hit the ball back before it bounces. This shot is called a volley.

A drop shot is a gentle tap that knocks the ball just over the net. The ball lands softly and doesn't bounce very high. If the opponent is not very close to the ball, he or she can't get to it in time.

A player working on her drop shot during a practice drill

A player pre-pares to hit an approaching lob shot (far left). A lob is often returned with a smash (left).

When a player hits a lob, the ball rises in a high arc over the opponent's head. The opponent may jump up in the air and try to smash it back over the net.

Making the Team

Although tennis began as a
recreational game, it has
become a fast-paced, action-
packed competitive sport.
There are junior competitions
and community tennis leagues.
High-school and college teams
compete with other schools
in local, state, and national

Sisters Serena and Venus Williams celebrate after winning the women's doubles championship at Wimbledon in 2002.

tournaments. The best tennis players in the world compete in international tournaments on the **professional** men's and women's tennis tours.

These professional tours organize dozens of tournaments in countries all over the world. Players travel from place to place to win titles, trophies, and prize money.

Most professional tennis tournaments include singles and doubles competitions. Men and women almost always play separately, but some tournaments have "mixed doubles" events. In mixed doubles, a man and a woman on one team

A professional mixed-doubles match

compete against a man and a woman on an opposing team.

For both men and women, four major tournaments are held each year: the Australian Open, the French Open, Wimbledon, and the U.S. Open. They are often called "Grand Slam" events because a player who has won all four of these **prestigious** events in the same year has won a "Grand Slam."

The French Open, which is played on clay courts, is one of four "Grand Slam" events in professional tennis.

It is extremely difficult to win a Grand Slam. The competition is intense. Players must compete successfully on several different surfaces— hardcourt, grass, and clay. They must also maintain a high level of play throughout the year.

In addition to the Grand Slam events, there are several international team competitions. Men represent their countries as they compete for

the Davis Cup. Women compete for the Fed Cup. Tennis became an Olympic sport in 1988.

The Grand Slam

Don Budge

To win a Grand Slam, a player must capture the Australian Open, the French Open, Wimbledon, and the U.S. Open all in the same year. In the history of the sport, only a few players have ever achieved this amazing feat. Don Budge became the first man to win a Grand Slam in 1938. "Rocket" Rod Laver won the Grand Slam in 1962 and again in 1969. Because he won *two* Grand Slams,

Rod Laver with his
U.S. Open trophy
in 1969

many people call Laver "the greatest player ever."

In 1953, Maureen Connolly became the first woman to win a Grand Slam. In 1988, Steffi Graf became the first player to win a "Golden Grand Slam." She captured all four major champi-onships, plus a gold medal at the Olympic Summer Games in Seoul, South Korea.

Steffi Graf with her Olympic gold medal

To Find Out More

Here are some additional resources to help you learn more about the game of tennis:

 **Books**

Blackall, Bernie. **Tennis.** Heinemann Library, 1999.

Italia, Bob. **100 Unforgettable Moments In Pro Tennis.** ABDO & Daughters Publishing, 1996.

Miller, Marc. **Fundamental Tennis.** Lerner Publications Company, 1995.

Reynolds, Keith. **Tennis.** Rigby Interactive Library, 1997.

Sanchez-Vicario, Arantxa. **The Young Tennis Player.** DK Publishing, Inc., 1996.

Organizations and Online Sites

Association of Touring Professionals / ATP Tour
200 ATP Boulevard
Ponte Vedra Beach, FL 32082
http://www.atptour.com

The ATP is the governing body of the men's professional tennis circuit.

International Tennis Federation
Palliser Road, Barons Court
London, England W14 9EN
http://www.itftennis.com

This organization is made up of national tennis associations from more than 198 countries. The ITF coordinates such major international competitions as the four Grand Slam tournaments, Olympic tennis, and the Davis Cup.

United States Tennis Association
70 West Red Oak Lane
White Plains, NY 10604
http://www.usta.com

The USTA exists to develop, coordinate and promote the game of tennis in the United States at both the amateur and professional levels.

Women's Tennis Association / WTA Tour
1266 East Main Street, 4th Floor
Stamford, CT 06902
http://www.sanexwtatour.com

The WTA is the governing body of the women's professional tennis circuit.

Important Words

boundaries lines that separate one area
from another

competitive eager to win

endurance ability to keep doing an activity

focused concentrating hard on something

opponents people one competes against

prestigious important, highly respected

professional referring to people who are
so good at something that they are paid
to do it

rally in tennis, a long exchange of shots

recreational done for fun

reflexes automatic responses

tournaments series of games in which
people compete to win championships

Index

(**Boldface** page numbers
indicate illustrations.)

ace, 20
Australian Open, 38, 42
Budge, Don, 42, **42**
Capriati, Jennifer, **41**
clay court, 12, **39,** 40
coaches, 30
Connolly, Maureen, 43, **43**
Davis Cup, 41
double fault, 20
doubles, 14
drills, 30, **30**
drop shot, 31, 33, **33**
fault, 19
French Open, 38, **39,** 42
Graf, Steffi, 43, **43**
Grand Slam, 39, 40, 42, 43
grass court, 12, 40
groundstroke, 31, 32, **32**
hardcourt, 12, 40
history of tennis, 5–10, **6, 9**
jeu de paume, 5
junior competitions, **2,** 35
Laver, Rod, 42, **42**
lob, 31, 34, **34**
mixed doubles, 37, **38**
net, 13, 16, 18, 21, 32, 33

Olympic tennis, 41, 43
Outerbridge, Mary, 8
rally, 20, **21**
Sampras, Pete, **41**
scoring, 17
serve, **1,** 18, 19, **19,** 20, 21,
    31, **31**
service court, 19
set, 15
singles, 14
smash, 31, 34, **34**
sphairistike, 7
Staten Island Cricket and
    Baseball Club, 9
tennis ball, 6, 7, 16, 18, 20,
    21, 22, **23,** 24, 28, 33
tennis clothes, 25–27, **25,**
    26
tennis court, 12, **13, 14,**
    16, 18, **19,** 27, **39**
tennis racket, 22, 23, **23,**
    28
U.S. Open, 38, 42
volley, 31, **32,** 33
Williams, Serena, **26, 36**
Williams, Venus, **36**
Wimbledon, **13,** 38, 42
Wingfield, Walter C., 7, 8,
    10

Meet the Author

Christin Ditchfield is the author of more than twenty books for children, including nine True Books on sports. A former elementary-school teacher, she is now a freelance writer, conference speaker, and host of the nationally syndicated radio program *Take It To Heart!* Ms. Ditchfield makes her home in Sarasota, Florida.